# MY FIRST
# ACTIVITY
# B·O·O·K

**ANGELA WILKES**

ALFRED A. KNOPF · NEW YORK

*For Sam*

**Design** Roger Priddy

**Photography** Dave King
**Art Editor** Chris Scollen
**Editor** Kate Woodward

Dorling Kindersley would like to thank Isobel Bulat, Amy Douglas, Nancy Graham, and Toby Spigel for their help in producing this book.

This is a Borzoi book published by Alfred A. Knopf, Inc.

First American edition, 1990

2  4  6  8  10  9  7  5  3  1

Library of Congress Cataloging-in-Publication Data
Wilkes, Angela. My first activity book by Angela Wilkes. p.cm.
Summary: Instructions for making masks, jewelry, Christmas tree decorations, and other objects from material readily available in the home. 1. Play—Juvenile literature. 2. Creative activities and seat work—Juvenile literature. [1. Handicraft.] I. Title.
HQ782.W45     1990     306.4′81—dc20     89-2640
ISBN 0–394–86583–9
ISBN 0–394–96583–3 [lib. bdg.]

# CONTENTS

# ACTIVITIES BY PICTURES

*My First Activity Book* shows you how to make all sorts of wonderful things from everyday materials you can find at home. Step-by-step photographs and simple instructions show you the materials you need and what to do with them. Everything is shown life-size so you can see exactly what the finished article will look like. On the opposite page is a list of things to do before you start, and below are the points you will find on each page to help you through the projects.

## How to use this book

### The things you need

All the materials for each project are shown life-size, to help you check that you have everything you need.

### Equipment

These illustrated checklists show you which equipment to have ready before you start making anything.

### Pattern pieces

There are pattern pieces to help you make some of the things in the book. All you have to do is trace them.

### CHRISTMAS TREE DECORATIONS

Add sparkle to your Christmas tree with shining angels, trees, and garlands made from nothing more than paper and ribbons. Make the decorations in red, blue, green, gold, and silver for a blaze of color. Turn the page to see the finished decorations.

**EQUIPMENT**

Ruler

Pencil

Scissors

Pinking shears

**You will need**

Fine colored ribbons

Shiny cardboard

Shiny wrapping paper

Glue stick

Tracing paper

Cellophane tape

Pattern pieces for decorations

Angel's wings

Angel's body

Christmas tree

Surprise cone

**Using a pattern piece**

Trace around a pattern piece and cut out the tracing.* Lay the tracing on a piece of cardboard and draw around it. Cut out the cardboard.

**Surprise cone**

Cut the cone pattern out of shiny paper. Roll it into a cone and glue the overlapping edge down. Glue on a loop of ribbon.

24

25

* Ask an adult to help you with the scissors.

# Things to remember

1 Cover your work table with newspaper before you start to make anything, unless the table has a wipeable top.

2 Put on an apron or old shirt to protect your clothes, and roll up your sleeves.

3 Read the instructions before you begin. Some of the activities take longer than others because things need time to dry.

4 Gather together everything you need, including the things shown in the equipment boxes.

5 Be very careful with sharp knives and scissors. **Do not use them unless an adult is there to help you.**

6 When you have finished, put everything away and clean up any mess.

## Step by step

Step by step photographs and clear instructions show you exactly what to do at every stage of the project.

## The final results

Life-size pictures show you what the finished projects look like, making it easy for you to copy them.

## Perfect presents

Many of the projects would make good presents. To find out how to wrap them, turn to pages 46 to 48.

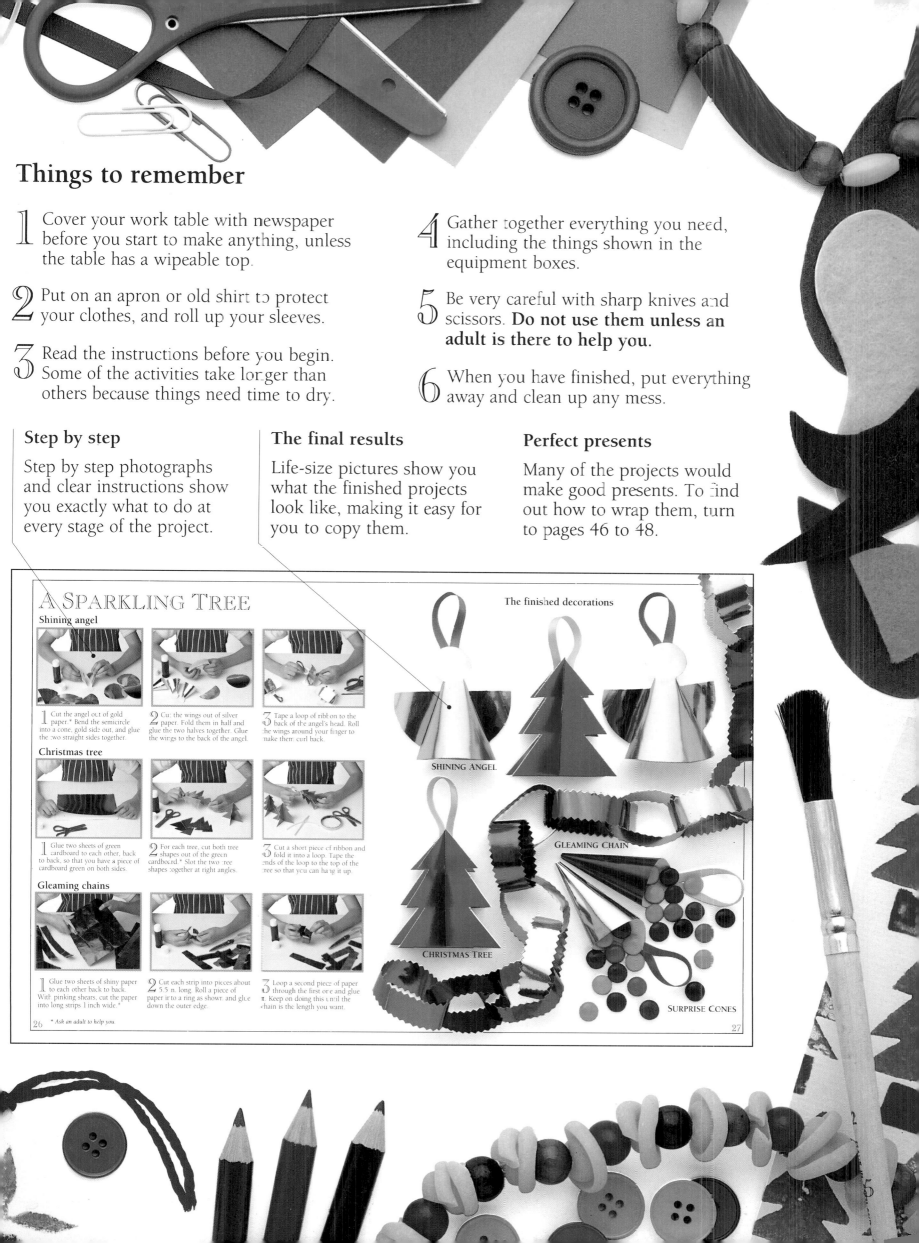

## A Sparkling Tree

The finished decorations

### Shining angel

1 Cut the angel out of gold paper.* Bend the semicircle into a cone, gold side out, and glue the two straight sides together.

2 Cut the wings out of silver paper. Fold them in half and glue the two halves together. Glue the wings to the back of the angel.

3 Tape a loop of ribbon on to the back of the angel's head. Roll the wings around your finger to make them curl back.

### Christmas tree

1 Glue two sheets of green cardboard to each other, back to back, so that you have a piece of cardboard green on both sides.

2 For each tree, cut both tree shapes out of the green cardboard.* Slot the two tree shapes together at right angles.

3 Cut a short piece of ribbon and fold it into a loop. Tape the ends of the loop to the top of the tree so that you can hang it up.

### Gleaming chains

1 Glue two sheets of shiny paper to each other back to back. With pinking shears, cut the paper into long strips 1 inch wide.*

2 Cut each strip into pieces about 5.5 in. long. Roll a piece of paper into a ring as shown and glue down the outer edge.

3 Loop a second piece of paper through the first one and glue it. Keep on doing this until the chain is the length you want.

SHINING ANGEL

GLEAMING CHAIN

CHRISTMAS TREE

SURPRISE CONES

26 * Ask an adult to help you.

27

# FANCY EGGS

Get out your paints, find some colored tissue paper, and you can surprise your family with colorful Easter eggs as bright as jewels.

Here and on the next two pages you can see how to cover eggs with colored tissue paper, paint patterns on them, and make them into little people.

## You will need

Colored tissue paper

Poster paints

Eggs (as many as you like)

Clear glue (with a fine nozzle)

Clear nail polish

Wallpaper paste

Scraps of yarn
(for little people)

Ribbon

### EQUIPMENT

Small bowl

Egg carton

Sewing needle

Pastry brush

Paintbrush

Jar of water

Scissors

# Emptying an egg

1 Hold the egg firmly and make a hole in the pointed end of it with the sewing needle.* Make a bigger hole at the other end.

2 Hold the egg over a small bowl. Blow hard into the small hole so that all the egg comes out of the big hole and drops into the bowl.

3 Rinse the egg clean under running water. Then dry it carefully and stand it, big hole downward, to drain until dry.

# Tissue paper eggs

1 For each egg you need a square piece of tissue paper about 8 in. long on each side. Tear the paper into pieces about 1 inch across.

2 Brush a thin coat of paste onto a piece of tissue paper. Stick the paper to the egg, smoothing it into place with your finger.

3 Keep on pasting paper to the egg until it is completely covered. Don't worry about pieces of paper overlapping or wrinkling.

# Painted eggs

4 Leave the tissue paper to dry.** Then paint the egg with clear polish.* Do one end first. Let it dry, then polish the other end.

1 Hold an egg carefully in one hand. Paint half of it, starting at one end. Keep the paint very thick and the patterns simple.

2 Let the first half of the egg dry, then paint the other half in the same way. When the whole egg is dry, polish it as shown before.

*Ask an adult to help you.

**This takes a few hours.*

# A NESTFUL OF EGGS

## Little people

  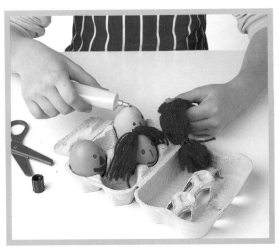

1 Paint a face on each egg. Use dots for the eyes, curved lines for the nose, mouth, and eyebrows, and blobs for the two cheeks.

2 To make hair, cut some strands of wool the same length as each other.* Tie them together with a shorter piece of wool.

3 Glue the wool to the top of the egg and arrange it to look like hair. You can cut bangs or perhaps tie a ribbon in it.

## TISSUE PAPER EGGS

*Pale-colored eggs, like the yellow one, need to be covered with two layers of tissue paper.*

*Using two colors of tissue paper, you can make patterned eggs.*

## PAINTED EGGS

*Use strong colors and simple, bold patterns such as stripes, zig-zags, or spots.*

## A FAMILY OF EGG PEOPLE

*Make each egg into a different character by using colored yarn for the hair. Try cutting it short or tying ribbons in it.*

Carrot top

Pigtail

Curly

*Ask an adult to help you with the scissors.*

9

# MAKING MASKS

For a special party, why not make yourself a mask and go in disguise! Or have a party with an animal theme and ask everyone to come wearing animal masks.

Here and on the next four pages you can find out how to make a chimp, a mouse, and an owl mask, all using the same basic pattern. You could also try making a mask of your own favorite animal.

## EQUIPMENT

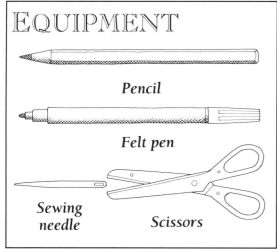

*Pencil*

*Felt pen*

*Sewing needle*

*Scissors*

## You will need

*Colored felt*

## Making the basic mask

1 Trace the mask pattern on the opposite page onto tracing paper. Cut out the tracing and carefully cut out the eyes.*

2 Glue the tracing onto thin cardboard and cut it out. Lay the cardboard mask on some felt, draw around it, and cut it out.**

3 Cut a piece of elastic long enough to go around the back of your head. Measure it from just in front of your ears.

*Ask an adult to help you with the scissors.*      ** *Look at the pictures on pages 14 and 15 to see which color to use.*

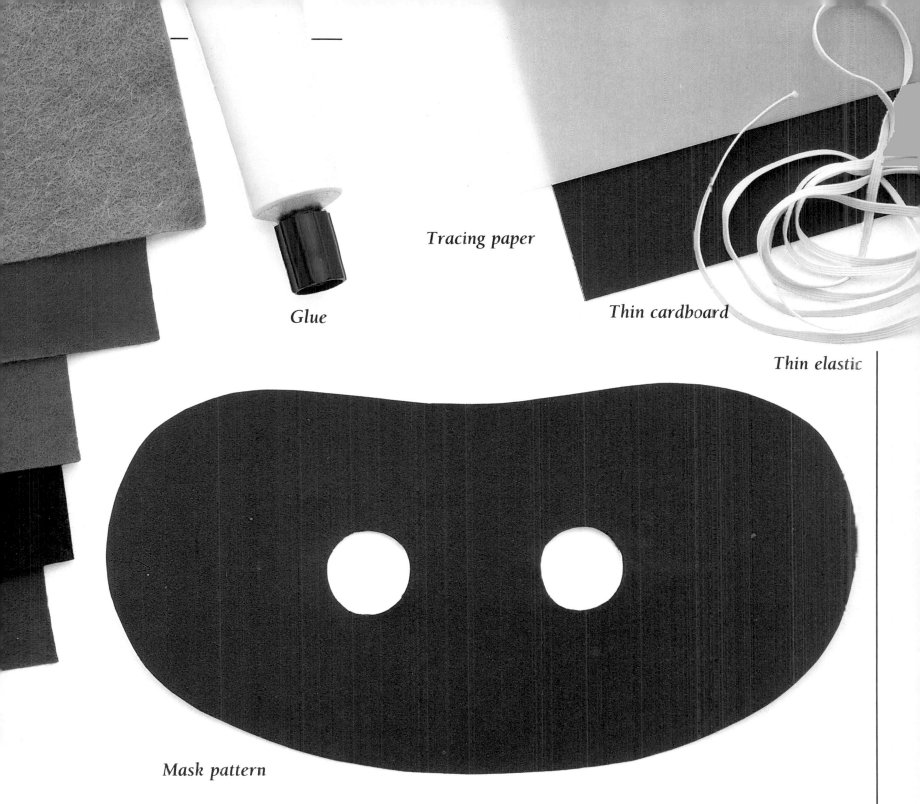

Tracing paper

Glue

Thin cardboard

Thin elastic

Mask pattern

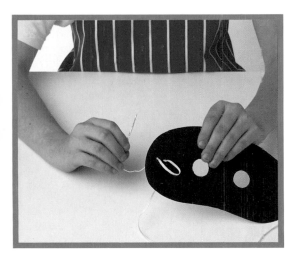

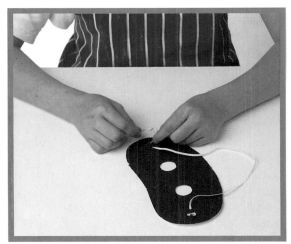

4 Tie a knot in one end of the elastic. Thread the other end onto a big needle. Make a stitch at one side of the cardboard mask.*

5 Pull the elastic tight. Loop it around the back of the mask and make a stitch at the other side of it. Knot the end of the elastic.

6 Dab glue on the front of the cardboard mask and stick the felt mask on top of it. Turn the page to see what to do next.

*Ask an adult to help you with the needle.*

11

# Making Faces

To make the basic mask into a chimp, an owl, or a mouse, just add different ears, eyes, noses, or a beak. Here all the extra pieces you need for each mask are shown life-size. All you have to do is trace the shapes to make pattern pieces. Check to see if the pieces need to be glued to cardboard.

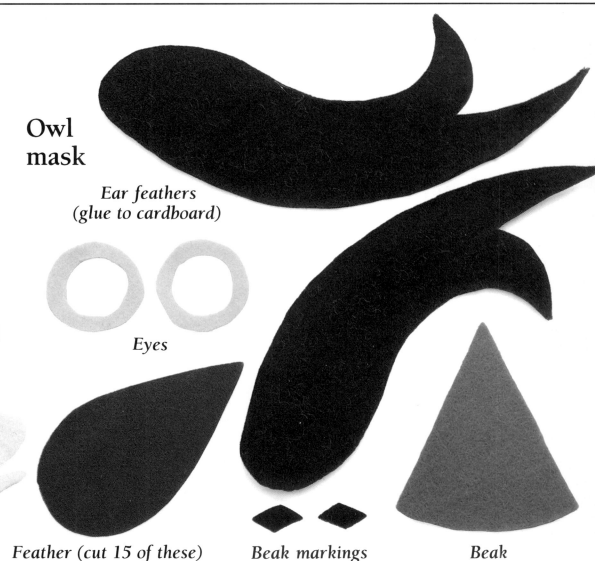

**Owl mask**

*Ear feathers (glue to cardboard)*

*Eyes*

*Strips for ear feathers*

*Feather (cut 15 of these)*

*Beak markings*

*Beak*

## Mouse mask

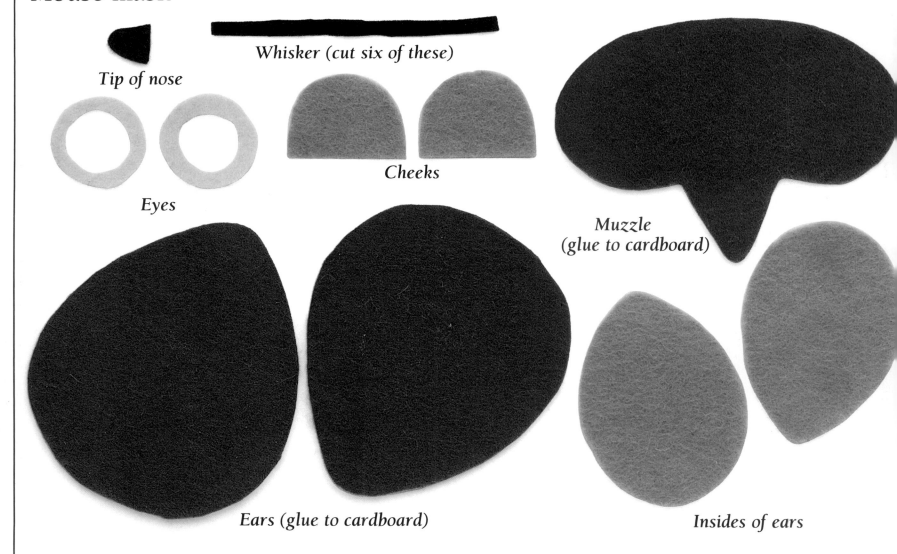

*Tip of nose*

*Whisker (cut six of these)*

*Eyes*

*Cheeks*

*Muzzle (glue to cardboard)*

*Ears (glue to cardboard)*

*Insides of ears*

# Chimp mask

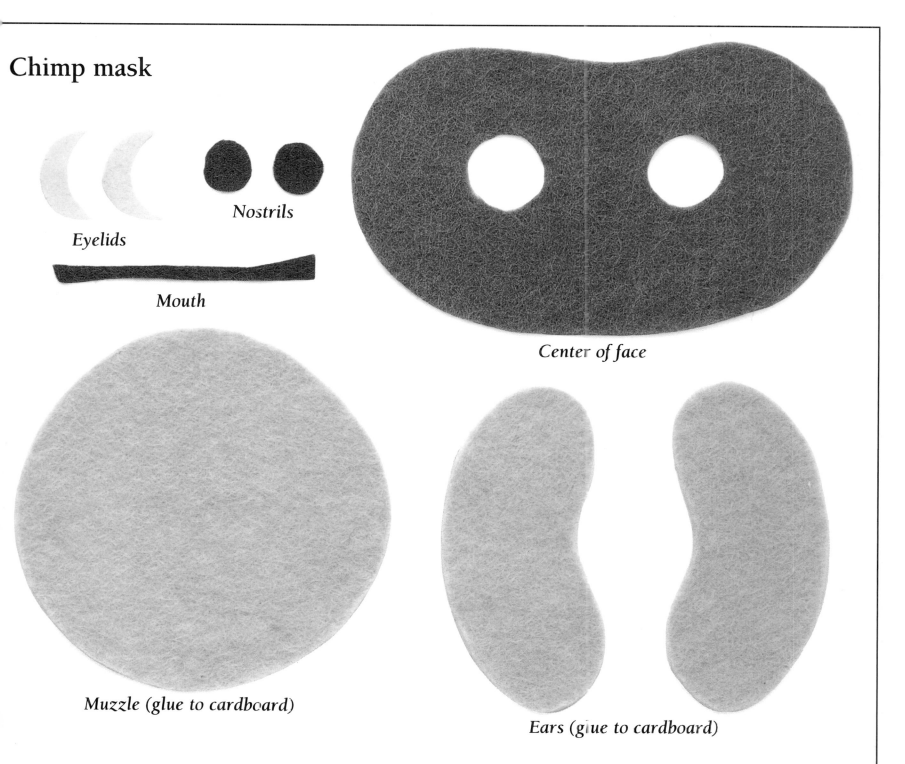

Eyelids

Nostrils

Mouth

Center of face

Muzzle (glue to cardboard)

Ears (glue to cardboard)

# Using the pattern pieces

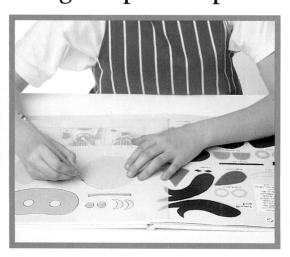

1 Choose the mask you want to make and trace around the pieces you will need. Cut the shapes out to make pattern pieces.*

2 Lay the pattern pieces on the felt you want to use. Draw around the pattern pieces and cut the shapes out of the felt.

3 Some shapes have to be glued to cardboard. Cut the cardboard out the same way as the felt. Glue them together.

* Ask an adult to help you with the scissors.

# MASQUERADE

Here are the finished masks! On the last four pages you saw how to make all the pieces you need for the masks. All you have to do now is put them together. Have your glue ready and follow these pictures and instructions.

## Chimp

*The basic mask for the chimp is dark gray. Glue the light gray felt in the middle of the mask, then glue on the muzzle. Glue the ears to the back of the mask at the sides. Last, glue on the nostrils, mouth, and eyelids.*

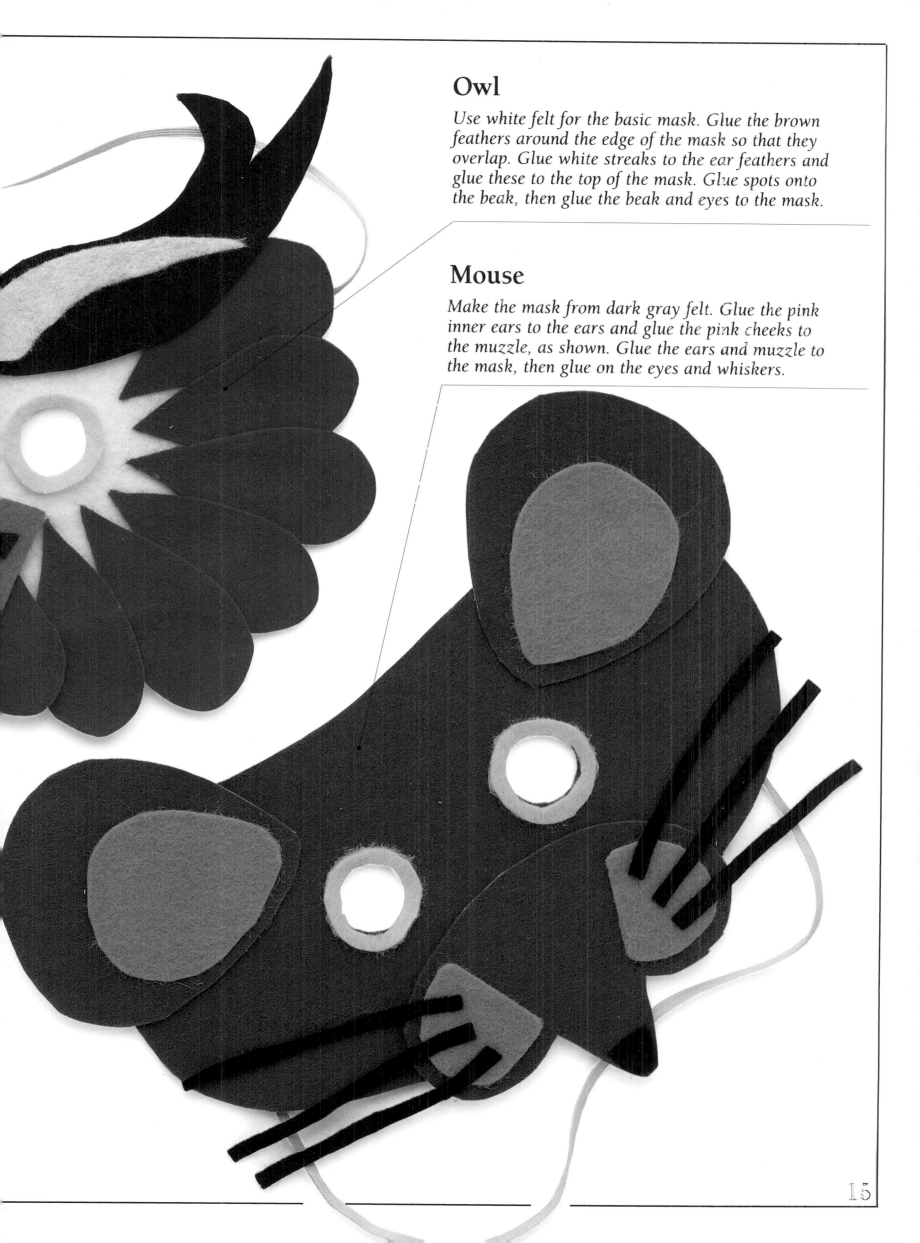

## Owl

*Use white felt for the basic mask. Glue the brown feathers around the edge of the mask so that they overlap. Glue white streaks to the ear feathers and glue these to the top of the mask. Glue spots onto the beak, then glue the beak and eyes to the mask.*

## Mouse

*Make the mask from dark gray felt. Glue the pink inner ears to the ears and glue the pink cheeks to the muzzle, as shown. Glue the ears and muzzle to the mask, then glue on the eyes and whiskers.*

15

# PASTA JEWELRY

Pasta is not just for eating! With a few handfuls of pasta rings, tubes, and bows, some bright poster paints, and multicolored ribbons and beads, you can make your own fancy jewelry. Try making a necklace in colors that will match your favorite blouse or skirt.

*Shirring elastic*

*Rolled elastic*

## You will need

*Pasta bows*

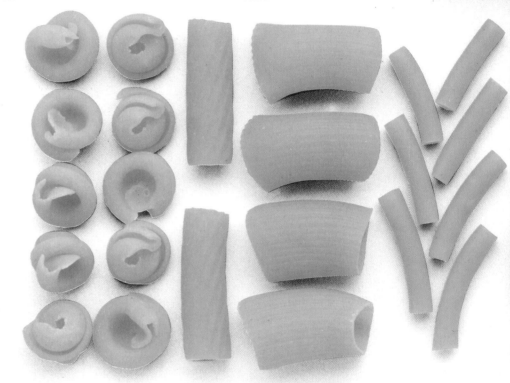

*Any pasta shapes with holes in the middle*

## Making a necklace

1 Paint some of the pasta shapes with thick poster paint. Paint tube-shaped pieces half at a time, letting them dry in between.

2 When the paint is completely dry, brush the pasta shapes with clear nail polish. Polish tubular shapes half at a time.

3 For a necklace using small pasta and beads, cut a piece of rolled elastic a little longer than you want the necklace to be.*

*Ask an adult to help you.*

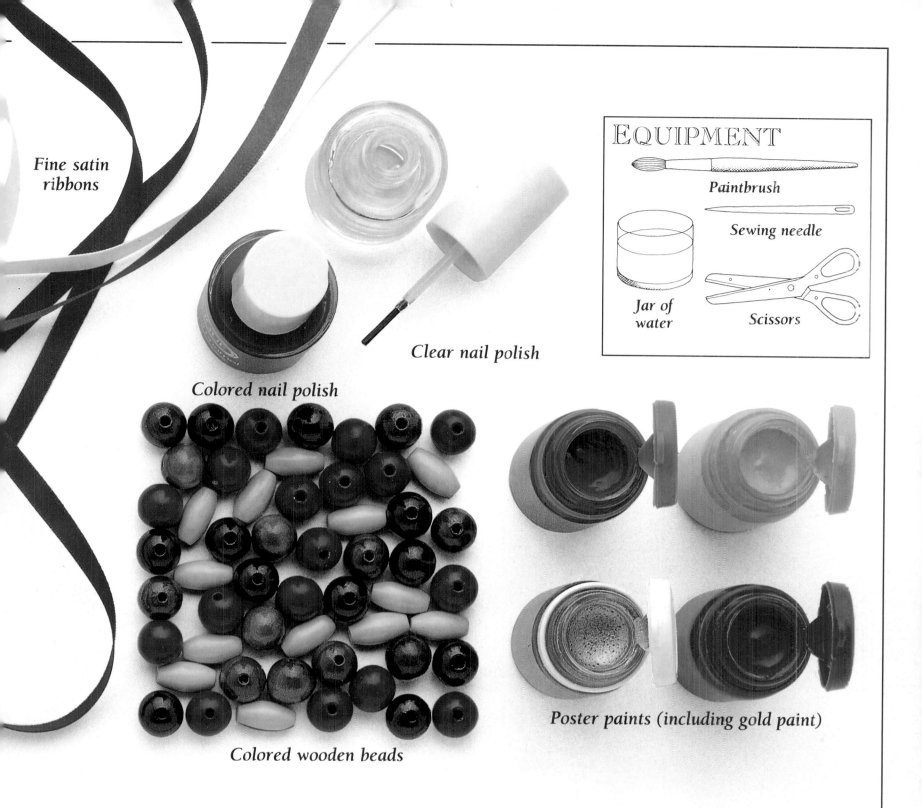

Fine satin ribbons

Clear nail polish

Colored nail polish

Paintbrush

Sewing needle

Jar of water

Scissors

Colored wooden beads

Poster paints (including gold paint)

4 Thread pasta and beads onto the elastic. You may need to use a big needle.* Tie the ends of the elastic in a knot.

5 Use shirring elastic to make necklaces from pasta bows. Thread the elastic through the tiny hole at the back of each bow.

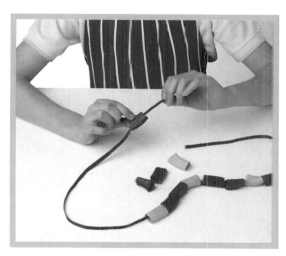

6 Thread large, chunky pasta shapes or beads onto a piece of ribbon. Tie the ends of the ribbon in a bow to complete the necklace.

* Ask an adult to help you.

# BOWS AND BEADS

Try making these necklaces or experiment with ideas of your own. Mix different types of pasta with contrasting beads and add brightly colored ribbon bows.

## JAZZY BRACELET

*Paint ribbed macaroni with dark pink nail polish. Thread onto elastic with green and yellow wooden beads.*

## RIBBONS AND BOWS

*Use plain macaroni, blue pasta bows, small red beads, and pink ribbon. Thread the macaroni and beads onto elastic and tie it. Then tie small pieces of ribbon around the pasta bows and tie them to the elastic between the macaroni.*

## BOBBLE BEADS

*For this necklace, use small pasta spirals and red, blue, and green wooden beads. You can make a matching bracelet using a shorter piece of elastic.*

18

## GOLD CHOKER

*Paint pasta bows
gold and thread them
onto shirring elastic
so that they overlap.*

## CHUNKY NECKLACE

*Use large pasta tubes
for this necklace. Thread
the pasta onto red ribbon and tie pieces
of white ribbon between each tube.*

# Paper Flowers

Paper flowers bloom brightly all year round and make good Christmas or birthday presents. Arrange them in a vase – without water – or tie them together with ribbon to make a bouquet.

Here and on the next two pages you can see how to make really lifelike roses, narcissus, and tulips. Once you can make these, try some others.

## You will need

*Clear glue in a tube with a fine nozzle*

*Cotton thread*

*Crepe paper*

*Cotton ball*

*Florist's wire*

*Thin wire*

# Making a rose

1 Cut a stem from florist's wire.* Cover one end with a tiny piece of cotton ball. Wrap and glue some pink crepe paper around it.**

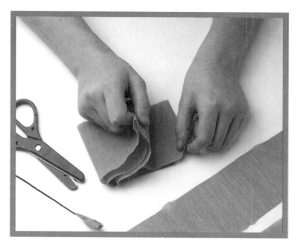

2 For the petals, cut a strip of pink crepe paper 31.5 in. by 3 in. Fold it in half lengthwise, then in half again three more times.

3 Cut the shape of a rounded petal top through all the layers of paper. When you open out the paper, you will have 16 petals.

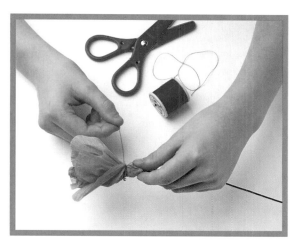

4 Wind the petals around the top of the wire stem. You can fold over the tops of the inner petals to make them more rose-like.

5 Tie cotton thread around the base of the petals. Then make two rosebuds the same way but half the size, to tie to the stem later.

## Making leaves

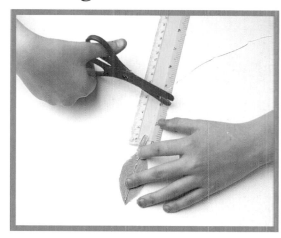

6 For each leaf cut two leaf shapes out of green crepe paper. Cut a piece of thin wire about 2 in. longer than the leaf.

7 Spread glue over one leaf shape. Lay the wire down the middle of it. Glue the second leaf on top to cover the wire.

8 Place the four leaves around the rose one at a time. Wind each of the four wires around the stem, to make them secure.

9 Wind a long strip of green paper around the rosebud stems and the main stem. Cover all the stem, then glue the end down.

*Ask an adult to help you with the scissors.*          **All stems should be prepared in this way.*

21

# A Paper Garden

## Making a narcissus

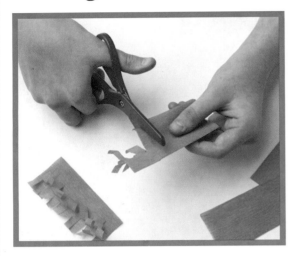 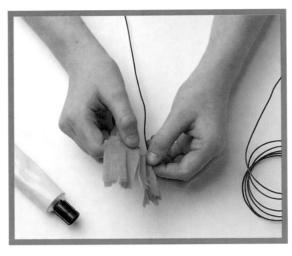 

1 For the center of the flower, cut a piece of orange paper 3.5 in. by 3.5 in. Fold it in half and snip along the edges to fringe them.*

2 Make a stem like the rose stem on the last page. Wind the orange center around the top of the stem and glue it in place.

3 Make white crepe paper petals and long, thin green leaves. Assemble the flower in the same way as the rose on page 21.

## Paper in bloom

*And here are the finished flowers. You can make an attractive display using all three types of flower or just one of them.*

**PINK ROSE**

**NARCISSUS**

**RED ROSE**

* Ask an adult to help you with the scissors.

# Making a tulip

1 To make the center, cut four strips of black crepe paper.* Twist them into loops and tie them to the top of a stem with thread.

2 Cut two small squares of yellow paper. Make a hole in the middle of them and push them up the stem as far as the black loops.

3 Cut five petals, each from red crepe paper 5 in. by 2.5 in. Tie them around the stem with thread. Finish the flower as before.**

**TULIP**

# CHRISTMAS TREE DECORATIONS

Add sparkle to your Christmas tree with shining angels, trees, and garlands made from nothing more than paper and ribbons. Make the decorations in red, blue, green, gold, and silver for a blaze of color. Turn the page to see the finished decorations.


## EQUIPMENT

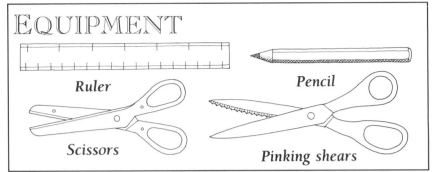

Ruler

Pencil

Scissors

Pinking shears

## You will need

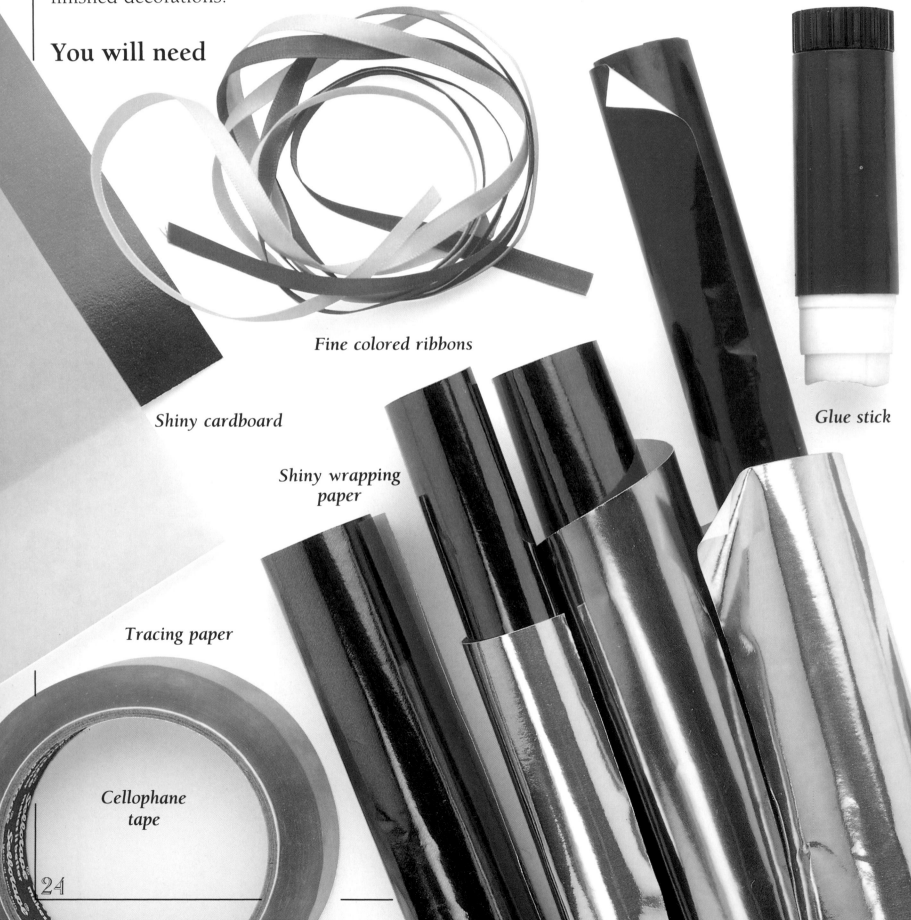

Fine colored ribbons

Shiny cardboard

Glue stick

Shiny wrapping paper

Tracing paper

Cellophane tape

24

# Pattern pieces for decorations

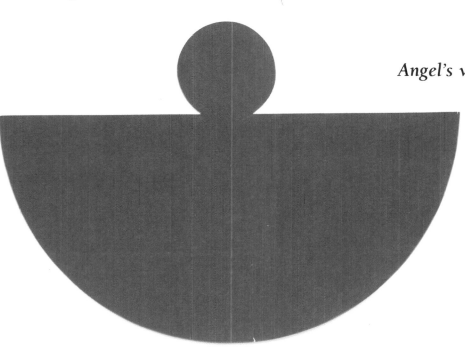

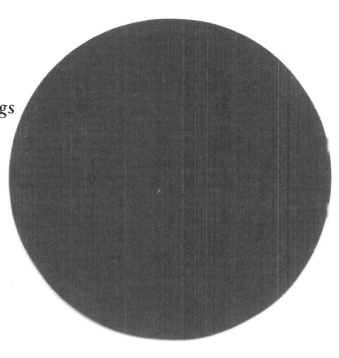

*Angel's wings*

*Angel's body*

*Christmas tree*

## Using a pattern piece

Trace around a pattern piece and cut out the tracing.* Lay the tracing on a piece of cardboard and draw around it. Cut out the cardboard.

## Surprise cone

Cut the cone pattern out of shiny paper. Roll it into a cone and glue the overlapping edge down. Glue on a loop of ribbon.

*Surprise cone*

* Ask an adult to help you with the scissors.

# A Sparkling Tree

## Shining angel

1 Cut the angel out of gold paper.* Bend the semicircle into a cone, gold side out, and glue the two straight sides together.

2 Cut the wings out of silver paper. Fold them in half and glue the two halves together. Glue the wings to the back of the angel.

3 Tape a loop of ribbon to the back of the angel's head. Roll the wings around your finger to make them curl back.

## Christmas tree

1 Glue two sheets of green cardboard to each other, back to back, so that you have a piece of cardboard green on both sides.

2 For each tree, cut both tree shapes out of the green cardboard.* Slot the two tree shapes together at right angles.

3 Cut a short piece of ribbon and fold it into a loop. Tape the ends of the loop to the top of the tree so that you can hang it up.

## Gleaming chains

1 Glue two sheets of shiny paper to each other back to back. With pinking shears, cut the paper into long strips 1 inch wide.*

2 Cut each strip into pieces about 5.5 in. long. Roll a piece of paper into a ring as shown and glue down the outer edge.

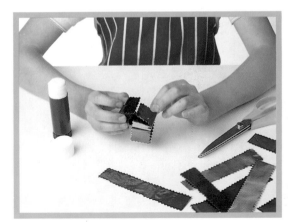

3 Loop a second piece of paper through the first one and glue it. Keep on doing this until the chain is the length you want.

*Ask an adult to help you.*

# The finished decorations

SHINING ANGEL

CHRISTMAS TREE

GLEAMING CHAIN

SURPRISE CONES

27

# ENVELOPE PUPPETS

Here and on the next two pages you can find out a really easy way to make puppets. Each puppet is made from an envelope big enough to go over your hand. Its features are made from cardboard, and details are added with household odds and ends. Why not invent your own puppets and put on a special puppet show with your friends!

## EQUIPMENT

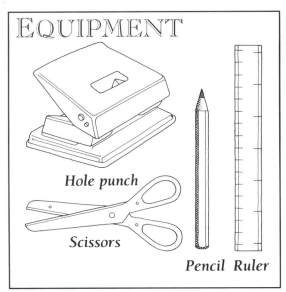

**Hole punch**

**Scissors**

**Pencil   Ruler**

## You will need

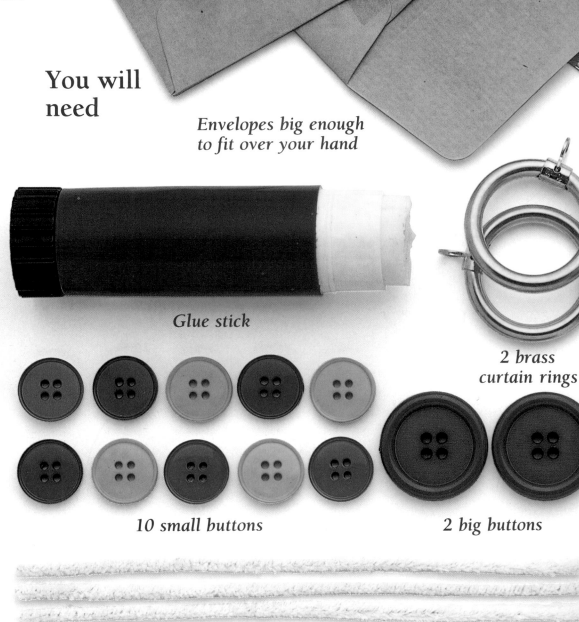

*Envelopes big enough to fit over your hand*

**Glue stick**

**2 brass curtain rings**

**10 small buttons**

**2 big buttons**

**3 pipe cleaners**

## Making a smiling clown

*1* Copying the clown on page 30, cut eyes, ears, mouth, hat, tie, suspenders, and shirt from cardboard.* Glue to envelope.

*2* Cut a sponge ball in half. Glue half of it, flat side down, in the middle of the envelope to make the clown's nose.

*3* For the hair, wind two coils of yarn around your hand, then attach both of them to the clown's head with paper clips.

*\* Ask an adult to help you with the scissors.*

Aluminum foil

Small sequins

Large sequins

Colored paper

2 sponge balls

2 paper clips

4 washers

Yarn

Gold braid

# Making a robot puppet

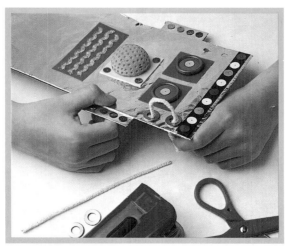

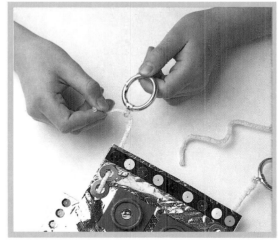

1 Glue aluminum foil around an envelope. Copy the picture on page 31 to make the robot's features and nose.

2 Put two washers onto a pipe cleaner and pull it through holes on the puppet's head. Make sure the washers cover the holes.**

3 Hook a curtain ring onto the top of each pipe cleaner. Then join the two curtain rings together with another pipe cleaner.

** *Do this on the other side of the puppet's head.*

*Turn the page to see how to complete the puppets.*

29

# HALLOWEEN LANTERNS

Traditionally, people carve lanterns out of pumpkins at Halloween to scare off witches and evil spirits. You do not have to have a pumpkin though. You can use a melon, a turnip, or a rutabaga and can transform them into magical lanterns in no time at all. Here you can see how to make your lantern, and the next two pages give you some more ideas on how to decorate them in different ways.

## You will need

*Small candles*

*Pumpkin*

*Green melon*

*Yellow melon*

*Use any one of these to make your lantern.*

## What to do

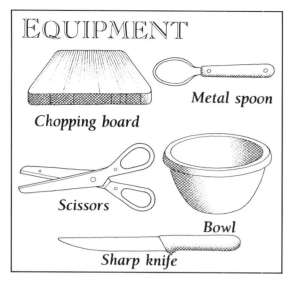

**Chopping board**
**Metal spoon**
**Scissors**
**Bowl**
**Sharp knife**

**Ball of string**

**Rutabaga**

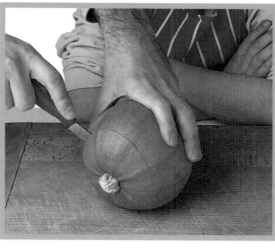

1 Ask an adult to slice off the top of your pumpkin with a sharp knife. The sliced-off piece will be the lid of the lantern.

2 Using the metal spoon, carefully scoop out the inside of the pumpkin. Try not to cut through the skin of the pumpkin.

3 Next, cut holes in the sides of the pumpkin.* Cut the holes to look like a face or just make a pattern (turn the page for ideas).**

4 Use the tip of the spoon to dig out a small hollow inside the base of the pumpkin. Wedge a candle firmly in the hollow.

5 Make two small holes near the top of the pumpkin. Thread a piece of string through them and knot the ends, to make a handle.

6 Cut a small hole in the lid of the pumpkin, to let out any smoke. Then ask an adult to light the candle for you.***

* Ask an adult to help you.
** Do not cut the holes too close together.

*** Do not try to light the candle yourself, because you might burn your fingers.

33

# LANTERN LIGHTS

These lanterns will shine out brightly on the darkest Halloween. They are made from pumpkins, melons, and rutabagas of all sizes and colors. Some have smiling faces and others have stars, moons, and other shapes cut out of them. Hang up your small lanterns and stand the big ones in a safe place on the ground. Have a spooky Halloween!

## GIANT PUMPKIN

*The giant pumpkin lantern is big enough to put two candles inside, so when they are lit, they look like two bright eyes.*

**SMILING RUTABAGA**

34

BABY PUMPKIN

SHINING YELLOW
MELON

BIG GREEN MELON

# PAPER POTTERY

You can make wonderful decorative bowls and plates with papier-mâché (mashed-up paper). The bowls and plates are made in stages and take a while to dry, so allow two days to make them. Here you can see how to make papier-mâché plates. On the next two pages you can find out the different ways to decorate them, and on pages 40 and 41 you can see the colorful results.

## You will need

## EQUIPMENT

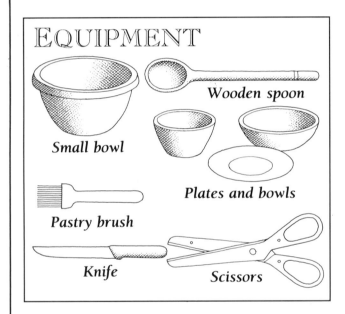

Small bowl

Wooden spoon

Plates and bowls

Pastry brush

Knife          Scissors

*Wallpaper paste\**

## What to do

**1** Tear lots of sheets of newspaper into strips about 1 inch wide. Then tear the strips into small rectangular pieces of paper.

**2** Spread petroleum jelly over the plate you are using as a mold.\*\* (You will need to spread it on the outside of a bowl.)

**3** Cover the plate with a layer of pieces of torn newspaper. Make the pieces of paper overlap each other so there are no empty spaces.

*\* Ask an adult to help you mix the paste.*                     *\*\* This keeps the papier-mâché from sticking to the mold.*

*Petroleum jelly*

*Lots of newspaper*

4 Brush wallpaper paste over the newspaper and cover it with another layer of newspaper. Leave this to dry for four to six hours.

5 Keep on doing this until there are six dry layers of papier-mâché. Separate the plate and the papier-mâché with a knife.\*\*\*

6 Trim the edge of the papier-mâché plate with scissors.\*\*\* Paste newspaper on the bottom of the plate over the petroleum jelly.

\*\*\* *Ask an adult to help you.*

37

# Decorating Papier-Mâché

Once your papier-mâché plates and bowls are completely dry, you can decorate them. Here are three different ways to do it. If you paint the bowls and plates, or if you cover them in tissue paper, it is best to use bold colors so the newspaper does not show through too much. You can decorate them to look like a matching set or make each one different.

**You will need**

## Equipment

*Bowl*

*Pastry brush*

*Saucer*

*Jar of water*

*Paintbrush*

*Pages from magazines*

*Papier-mâché bowls or plates*

*Poster paints*

*Clear nail polish*

## Painting the plates

**1** Paint a pattern on your plate or bowl, using thick poster paint. Paint light colors first and try not to let them run into each other.

**2** When the paint is completely dry, brush a coat of clear polish all over it to make it shine.* Let the polish dry completely.

## Patchwork plates

**1** Tear brightly colored pages from magazines into strips about 1 inch wide. Then tear each strip into smaller pieces of paper.

**2** Paste the pieces of paper onto the plate or bowl so that they overlap a little. Let the paper dry, then polish it, as shown above.

## Tissue paper plates

**1** Tear pieces of tissue paper into strips about 1 inch wide. Then tear the strips into smaller rectangular pieces of paper.

**2** Paste the pieces of tissue paper to the plate or bowl. Paste on two layers of paper and leave it to dry, then polish it, as above.*

*\* Ask an adult to help you.*

*Wallpaper paste*

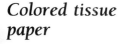

*Colored tissue paper*

39

# LOTS OF POTS

Here are the finished plates and bowls. The painted ones are all done in the same colors, which makes them look like a set even though they all have different patterns. The tissue paper plates are covered in brightly colored tissue paper, and the patchwork ones in a mosaic of magazine paper.

**TISSUE PAPER PLATE AND BOWL**

**PATCHWORK PLATE AND BOWL**

40

PAINTED PLATES

41

# PRINTING PRESS

Even the tiniest present looks special if it is wrapped in handmade paper. You can print your own original wrapping paper and gift tags using the simplest everyday objects, such as potatoes and leaves. Here and on the next two pages you can find out how to do potato and leaf prints, and make stencils for printing. Cover your work table with newspaper and start your very own printing press.

## You will need

*Colored tissue paper*

*Thin cardboard*

*White paper*

*Black cardboard*

*Leaves (for leaf prints)*

*Potatoes (for potato prints)*

*Poster paints*

*Sponge (for stencils)**

*Yarn for tags*

### EQUIPMENT

Paintbrush

Sharp knife

Scissors

Pencil

Chopping board

Saucer

\* With an adult's help, cut small pieces from a regular-sized sponge. Cut a piece for each color

# Christmas tree potato prints

1 Cut a potato in half.** On one half of the potato draw a tree shape. Cut away the potato around the tree to make it stand out.

2 Mix some green paint with a little water in a saucer. Press the cut potato into the paint, then down onto a big piece of paper.

3 Make tree prints all over the paper. Cut a pot out of the other half of the potato. Use red paint to print pots under the trees.

## GIFT TAGS

For gift tags, do single prints on small pieces of cardboard. Make a hole in the corner of each one and tie a piece of yarn through it.

## PRINTED PAPER

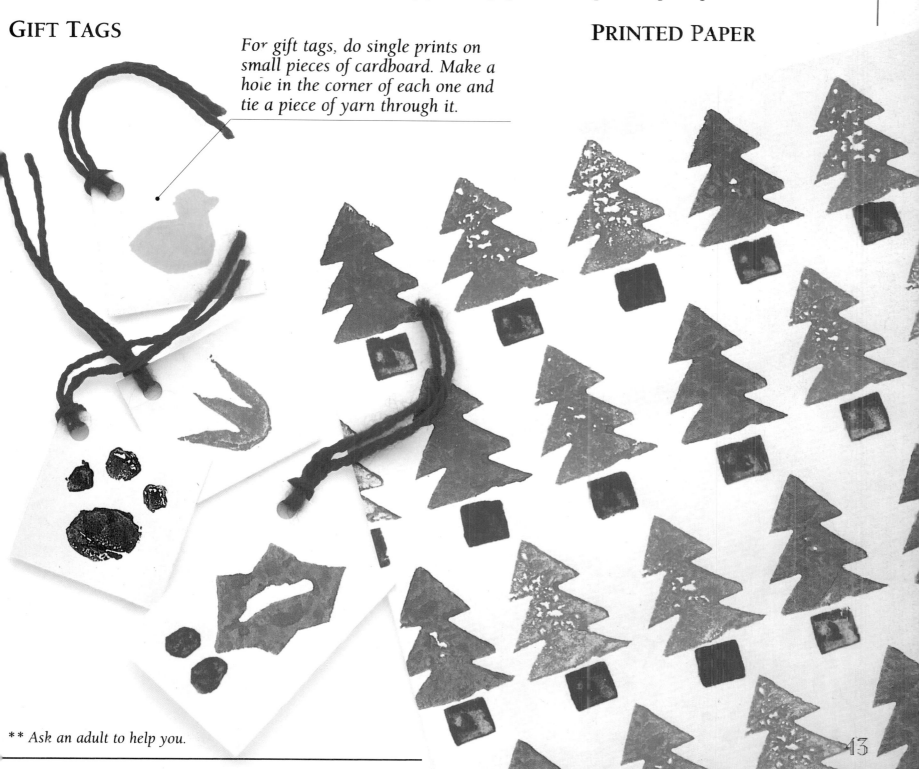

** Ask an adult to help you.

43

# SIMPLE PRINTS

## Stenciled tulip paper

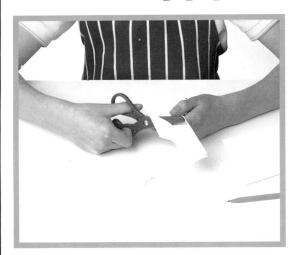  

1 Fold a piece of cardboard in half. Draw half a tulip and a leaf on one side and cut them out.* Open the cardboard.

2 Mix thick poster paint in saucers. Hold the stencil flat on paper. Dab the sponge in pink paint, then over the cut-out tulip.

3 Dab another piece of sponge in green paint, then over the cut-out leaves. Lift the stencil carefully off the paper.

4 Repeat the stencils to make a tulip pattern all over the paper. Use a single stencil print to make gift tags. Try using different colors and making other stencils, like the apple below.

44   *Ask an adult to help you.*

# Leaf prints

  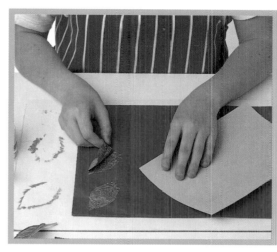

1 Lay a fresh, non-evergreen leaf down on newspaper and paint one side of it with thick poster paint straight from the pot.

2 Lay the leaf face down on a big piece of paper. Cover the leaf with a piece of scrap paper and rub across it with your fist.

3 Lift off the scrap paper, then the leaf. Do more prints the same way all over the paper, painting the leaf each time.

## SHINING LEAVES

*Here is another idea for your printing press. Brush gold poster paint over different-shaped leaves. Print them on colored tissue paper or cardboard.*

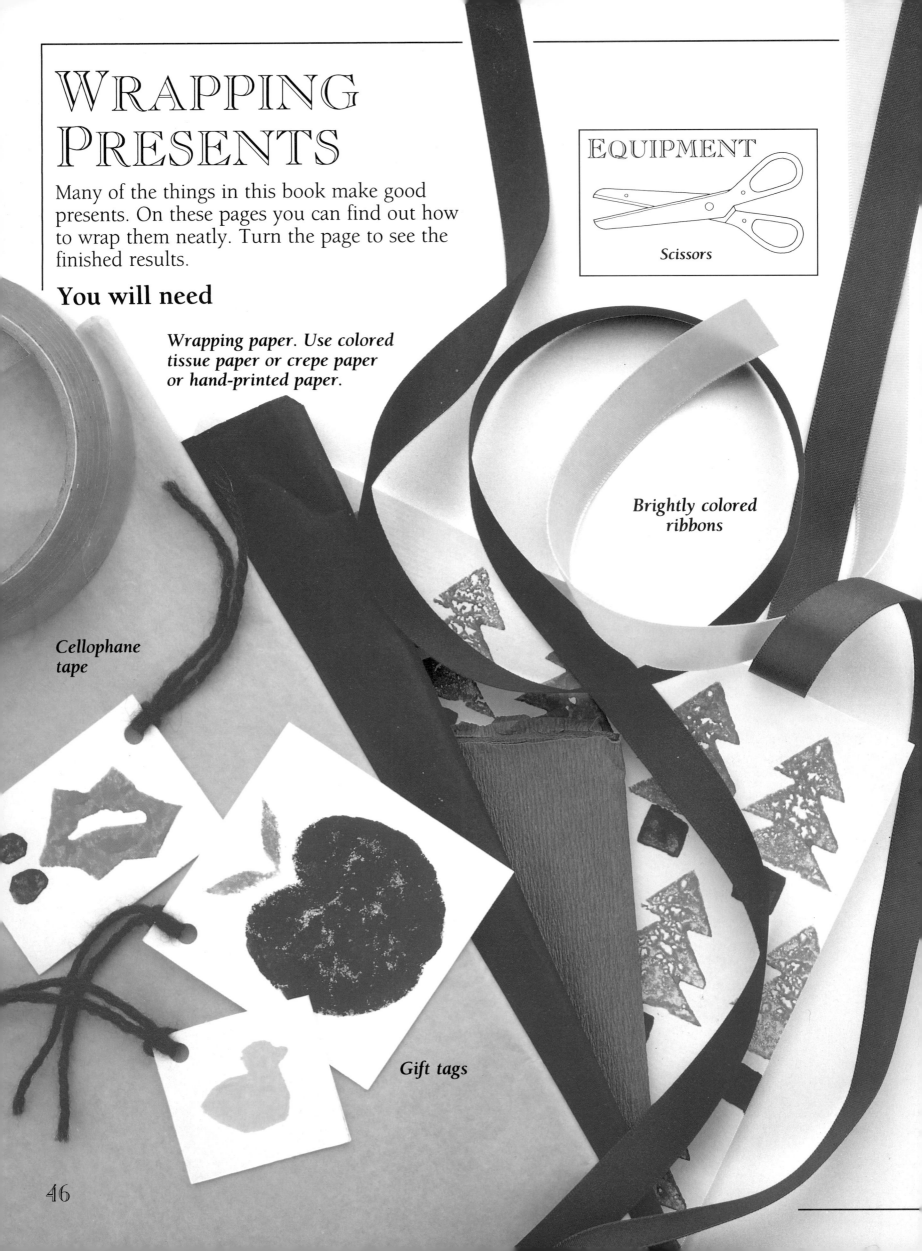

# WRAPPING PRESENTS

Many of the things in this book make good presents. On these pages you can find out how to wrap them neatly. Turn the page to see the finished results.

## You will need

*Wrapping paper. Use colored tissue paper or crepe paper or hand-printed paper.*

*Brightly colored ribbons*

*Cellophane tape*

*Gift tags*

# Rectangular present

1 Cut a piece of paper big enough to wrap right around the present and overlap it.* Put the present in the middle of the paper

2 Hold one side of the paper over the present. Then fold the other half over it so that it overlaps. Stick it down with cellophane tape.

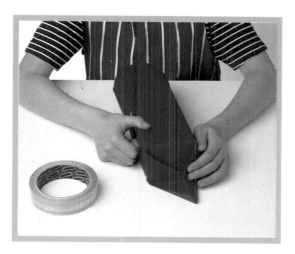

3 Fold down the end of the paper to cover one end of the present. Fold in the flaps at each side so that they lie flat.

4 Fold in the pointed flap of paper and tape it down. Turn the present around and fold in the other end in the same way.

5 Cut a long piece of ribbon. Lay it under the present and bring the ends over the top. Loop them around each other and pull tight.

6 Turn the present over. Wrap the ribbon around it, threading the ends under the first piece. Tie them in a bow and tape on a gift tag.

# Tubular present

1 Cut a piece of paper 8 in. longer than the present. Roll the present up in the paper and tape down the overlapping edge.

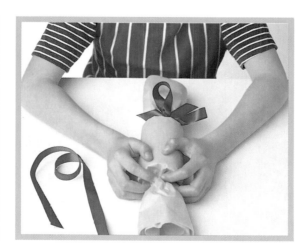

2 Scrunch up the paper at each end of the present, to make it look like a party popper. Tie a piece of ribbon around each end in a bow.

3 Cut small triangles out of the paper at the ends of the present to give it zigzag edges. Then tape on a gift tag.

*If you are using tissue paper, use a piece folded in half so that it is double thickness. Ask an adult to help you with the scissors.*

47

# FINISHING TOUCHES

For the brightest presents, use wrapping paper and ribbons in contrasting colors and your own homemade gift tags.

48